Author : Prisha Laskar

Illustrated by : Gopal lohar

We offer stories, coloring books and activity books about Indian Culture and Festivals

Contact Us At :

prishalaskar@gmail.com

And get your kid next copy, of our products at 70% OFF

Stay Tuned !!

Prisha Laskar

It was the time of the year when the school announces a two-week holiday after the weekly exams are over and Arya can finally take a break from books.

Last night Arya had eavesdropped on his parent's conversations about flying to their native hometown, India, during this holiday. They were talking about spending Diwali with everyone back in their hometown.

Though Arya's nationality was Indian, he was born and raised in the States, making the kid grow attached to the foreign country more than his motherland. And following this, the boy knew more about American festivals rather than Indian ones.

When his parents discussed Diwali, Arya had little to no clue how the festival is spent or what the festival is about. Yes, he indeed came across some school books on Diwali calling it the festival of lights, but Arya couldn't remember further than that. Well, he wasn't that much of a bright student.

"Hey!" Arya got startled when a voice surprised him from behind. The kid glared at his group of friends, whom all had mischievous smiles on their faces.

"Marie was planning that we spend the weekend in her farmhouse," Evan informed while he sat on the empty swing beside Arya.

"I don't think I can make it this year," Arya announced with a sad face gaining the full attention of his friends.

"Why?" Marie, Evan, Luke, and Emma all chirped in simultaneously with curiosity.

"Mom and dad are planning a trip to India this week. The upcoming week is Diwali, so they want to spend that with other family members." Arya spoke with a disheartened look on his face. He didn't want to leave his friends and go back.

"What's Diwali?" Marie asked with curiosity.

"It's a festival just like our Christmas, or Thanksgiving, or Easter. It mainly falls in November and is celebrated all across India. Diwali is also known as the festival of lights cause houses are decorated with clay lamps and candles, and firecrackers are burst everywhere. Am I right, Arya?" Evan spoke, making everyone speechless and surprised.

Arya was the Indian one, but Evan looked like the one who was the real Indian to the twelve-year-old kid.

He knew more than Arya knew about Diwali. For the first time, Arya felt jealous of his friend.

"Wow, Evan! Where did you even learn this from?" Luke patted the other's shoulder and asked.

Evan let out a small smile and muttered, "News. Also, my dad had this Indian friend who used to talk the whole time of the festivals celebrated there."

"So, Arya, that means you will be spending the holiday celebrating Diwali? That's cool!" Emma inquired while Arya simply nodded.

Soon school was over, and Arya walked to his house in a sour mood.

"No, mom. Yeah, I know. I am sorry. It's just that we got a new deal today, and the boss has asked all of us to start working overtime. Next year I promise we will be there."

Arya heard his father's voice as soon as he stepped inside the house coming from the living room. He slowly peeked his head inside and saw his parents sitting on the sofa and talking with his grandma through video call.

"Grandma!" Arya burst inside the living room when the kid saw his grandma's face on the laptop screen. He missed his grandma.

"Look who's here. Arya, my child, how are you?" Grandma beamed with delight after Arya's face moved closer to the laptop screen. "I am good, grandma. How are you? How is grandpa?" "Everyone is fine. Your grandpa is busy giving instructions to the decorators outside. Diwali is coming and with all the preparations....... I was so excited to meet my grandchild after so many years, but I guess I've to wait for another year."

" Arya grew confused after listening to his grandma. He gave his dad a quizzical look. "I promise I will make the reunion happen next year."

Arya's father gave his words of assurance and excused himself when he got a call from his boss. Arya saw his grandma trying to hide her sadness behind her smile.

"Mom, you talk with Arya. I am gonna go finish my laundry." Arya's mom excused herself too, leaving the grandma and her grandchild to have all the time in the world.

"Grandma, can I ask something?" Arya shifted in his seat and asked with hesitation. "Sure, my child." Arya smiled, hearing his grandma using such endearments. It made him feel that they were so close and not in two separate states.

"How will you describe Diwali? I mean, what's it important for? I've read in books that it's called the festival of lights, but as someone who hadn't celebrated it ever, I want to hear it from you who has so much experience regarding the occasion." Arya finished, and he could see his grandma grinning at him, her eyes shining with excitement.

"I am glad that you asked this, Arya. As an Indian, it's imperative to know your roots. No matter where we are, we should always remember where we belong from," Grandma said and then started explaining to her grandchild the meaning of Diwali.

"Diwali is mostly known as the festival of lights, but what it is mainly celebrated for is bringing happiness, prosperity, and health in one's life. There are five days of Diwali. The first day is called Dhanteras. On this auspicious day, we perform Goddess Laxmi Puja. We buy gold or silver product on this day as it is believed that they protect us from bad omen. The next day is known as Choti Diwali, where we perform puja to protect the family and our loved ones from evil eyes. Families gather together to lit diyas and candles and then proceed to burst crackers. The third day is the main day of Diwali. Lord Ganesha and Maa Laxmi puja is held on this day, and people share blessings, sweets, and gifts. And then, on the fourth day of Diwali, we perform Govardhan Puja. On this day, Lord Krishna defeated Indra by lifting the Govardhan mountain. People worship this day by making a small hillock using cow dung which symbolizes the Govardhan mountain. The fifth and the last day is called Bhai Dooj. On this day, sisters pray for their brother's long and happy life while sweets and gifts are shared. Every day holds a special meaning Arya, but what brings them together is the victory of good over evil and light over darkness, so my grandchild don't forget to light your candle when Diwali arrives."

Arya was left amazed. His grandma explained everything so beautifully and easily, which the books couldn't even do.

"Thanks, grandma. You explained better than my school teachers." Arya and his grandma both laughed at the remark when an idea struck the kid's head.

"Grandma, I have an idea." Arya then proceeds to explain his idea to his grandma, whose smile grew more prominent at each passing second hearing the little one's plan.

"Great plan. Go and show everyone how Diwali is celebrated." With grandma's blessings and good luck, Arya cut the call and ran out of the room to tell his parents about the plan.

"Mom, Dad, why don't we celebrate Diwali here? I mean when we can't go to India why don't we just bring the festival here. We can also invite our friends. It will be fun."

Arya's dad and mom stopped doing their respective works when their son announced his brilliant idea. It was a good suggestion. To celebrate the festival altogether. "That's a nice thought. We can arrange that."

Arya jumped in joy when his dad approved the idea, and his mom, too, gave him a thumbs up. The kid can't contain his excitement to celebrate Diwali with his friends.

As planned, Arya and his parents got busy decorating their house and sent out invitations. One week passed in a blink, and the day of the main festival arrived.

"Arya, where have you kept the box of sweets?" Arya's mom called out to her son, who came running down the stairs dressed in a traditional kurta and pajama set. This is the first time in Arya's life that he was wearing Indian wear, and somehow, he loved it. "

"I kept it in the fridge, mom. On the upper left." Arya saw his mom wearing a beautiful rose pink saree while his father, who was busy talking with the caterers, wore a kurta and pajama just like him.

Their pleasantly decorated house with garlands and chandeliers, his parents wearing Indian wear, his grandma sending sweets from India, and holding a puja made Arya feel that he was in his own country. The feeling was surreal to the little kid.

"Arya, look whom all came." Arya's dad said and stood aside so that Arya can take a look at the guests. There were his friends standing with gifts in their hands and smiles on their faces. Arya was ecstatic.

He ran towards his group and welcomed them with hugs. Soon, more guests started to arrive, and Arya's house was filled with laughter and gossip. All of the guests had similar expressions on their faces: amused.

"Wow, buddy, I have read about Diwali in books, but how the festival is celebrated right before my eyes, it's completely a different feeling," Evan spoke, making Arya's other friends nod their heads in agreement.

Arya felt proud hearing it. His friends and everyone acknowledged their tradition with such amusement and joy that Arya and his parents were filled with satisfaction.

The celebration was a success. As neighbors and people, Arya and his family bonded well with everyone, and the guests too asked the family to hold such a festival every year.

At the time of farewell, Arya hugged his friends and thanked them for their presence.

Before walking out, Evan whispered into Arya's ears, "Look out of your window at the evening. We have a surprise for you."

Arya was startled. What more is left? They had gotten him so many gifts, so he hesitated at first, but when his friends requested him to just follow the plan, Arya couldn't say no.

"Mom, dad, Evan said that he and the others have one more surprise for us. He told me to look out of the window when it starts to get dark."

The family quickly moved near the windows and were left stunned. Every house in their area was lit up with different lights. Some pulled out their Christmas trees and decorated them with lights. Some brightened up their entrances with dreamy fairy lights, while some used curtain LED lights. Arya looked to his right and saw a giant Christmas tree outside Evan's house embellished with small colorful lights.

"What's all this?" Arya's dad, who was left puzzled and surprised, asked his wife, who was as clueless as him.

"I think I know. Evan earlier told me that people here know Diwali as the festival of lights, so I think it's their way of honoring the festival."

Arya said while his parents were shocked. They couldn't believe someone would do that for them. For a festival which wasn't even theirs.

But unlike his parents, Arya was calm and composed. His grandma told him that what brings everyone together are unity and love, and today, Arya felt that. He saw that through the small gesture his neighbors attained to show.

Growing up as a kid who had never visited his motherland, Arya was clueless about Diwali's celebration. So, when the kid learns that his parents are planning to visit India to participate in the festival, Arya wasn't thrilled. Realizing that his American friend knows more about his culture than he did, Arya goes to his home and seeks help from his grandma, who lives in India. Later, when the kid finds out that they can't travel to India due to his dad's office work, Arya plans with his grandma to hold the festival back in the foreign land. Invitations were sent, and everything was prepared for the celebration. All guests were thrilled to learn about a new cultural festival and enjoyed the day together. Arya, who had no knowledge about Diwali, with his grandma's help, discovered the true meaning of the festival; unity and love.

The End

Firecrackers

Diya

Decorations

Saree

Kurta

Marigold

Vocabulary

Rangoli

Laddu

We offer stories, coloring books and activity books about Indian Culture and Festivals

Contact Us At :

prishalaskar@gmail.com

And get your kid next copy, of our products at 70% OFF

Stay Tuned !!

Prisha Laskar